John Kendrick Bangs

A Prophecy and a Plea

Being First a Stygian Prophecy and Second a Plea for Naturalism Two

Poems Read on Diverse Occasions

John Kendrick Bangs

A Prophecy and a Plea
Being First a Stygian Prophecy and Second a Plea for Naturalism Two Poems Read on Diverse Occasions

ISBN/EAN: 9783744769693

Printed in Europe, USA, Canada, Australia, Japan

Cover: Foto ©ninafisch / pixelio.de

More available books at **www.hansebooks.com**

A PROPHECY AND A PLEA

BEING FIRST A STYGIAN PROPHECY
AND SECOND A PLEA FOR NATU-
RALISM . . . TWO POEMS
READ ON DIVERS
OCCASIONS

BY

JOHN KENDRICK BANGS

PRIVATELY PRINTED
AT NEW YORK, ANNO DOMINI ONE THOU-
SAND EIGHT HUNDRED AND NINETY-SEVEN

CONTENTS

There were sinful souls about me, men
    too wicked e'en to go
O'er the inky stream to Hades where
    the furnaces are kept,
And some shrieked aloud profanely as
    they wandered to and fro,
While some others on the pier front
    gnashed their spirit teeth and wept.

And although I am not timid as a rule, I
    must admit
When I thought of how these spirits
    swarming up and down the shore
Were too vile for them in Hades—if one
    can imagine it—
All my nerves were in a flutter and my
    heart was sick and sore.

2

They would potter all about me, they
 would grimace in my face;
They would terrify my optics and
 they'd horrify my ears:
I'd have parted with a fortune for a
 chance to leave the place,
And escape the horrid visions that had
 so aroused my fears.

Now perhaps I should explain it, how I
 happened to be there:
I was not a finished mortal like those
 other sorry souls,
I was not a footsore climber of the so-
 called golden stair;
But had gone by invitation where the
 inky river rolls.

3

I'd received a note from Boswell, rather,
    word by telephone—
How the deuce he made connections I
    as yet don't understand,
But the word came o'er the wires in a
    deep profundo tone,
" We've a meeting at the House-boat—
    would you like to be on hand ?"

I had answered, " Would I ? Rather !
    What's to be the style of night?
Story-tellers, or the poets, or a chafing-
    dish instead ?"
" 'Tis a meeting of the prophets," he re-
    plied, " of prophets bright,
Who will tell us what is coming in the
    centuries ahead.

4

"Old Isaiah has a notion that there's
    lots of fun to come,
And Cassandra has a poem that we're
    going to let her read;
Jeremiah's got a paper that will strike
    you mortals dumb
With a vision of the future that we
    think you'd better heed."

Who would not be interested in an
    evening of that kind ?
Who would not receive a warning of the
    future if he could ?
Who would lose a chance like this one
    to improve his narrow mind,
In despite of all the terrors of that hor-
    rorific wood ?

So I jumped aboard the cable and I rode
  for many a mile,
And I stuck to it right sternly till I
  ` reached the hither bank
Of the unpellucid river where the people
  seldom smile,
Of the river that of rivers is the fumidest
  and dank.

Then at last, with much of hailing, boat-
  man Charon reached the pier
On a sort of combination of canal-boat
  and a yacht,
And I asked him what his fare was, and
  he scratched his ancient ear
As he answered to my question, "I
  dunno, sir, whatcher got?"

6

And I beg you'll understand me when I
    say that he said that—
'Tis a rather free translation of the
    words that he did speak;
For we know of course that Charon in
    such English isn't pat,
And his only known vernacular is plain
    Homeric Greek.

Furthermore it must be stated in behalf
    of Charon's self,
Lest I seem to give the notion that the
    chap was full of tricks,
There's a tariff down in Hades that ex-
    cludes all foreign pelf
And there's never been a mortal got his
    money o'er the Styx.

They may take an arrant pauper on that
    other mystic shore,
They may take a lot of folks in who like
    Turpin shone for stealth ;
But they've built a Chinese wall there
    that contains no single door
To admit an aristocracy that's founded
    on mere wealth.

When I'd answered that I'd nothing
    Captain Charon arched his brows—
"Then I fear I cannot take you," he
    replied and turned away ;
"I'm not in the ferry business for the
    fun of running scows,
And unless you'd like to swim it I'm
    afraid you'll have to stay."

Then a voice came o'er the river broad
and deep—a triple base,
Through a Megaphone arrangement
bringing out each single note :
"Stop your jewing !—row him over,
'less you want to lose your place.
He's to be our guest this evening at the
meeting on our boat."

"Very well, Sir Walter Raleigh," an-
swered Charon turning pale ;
"I was not aware this person was a
friend of yours, My Lord.
I will break the record with him if it
takes a ripping gale."
And he turned and said urbanely,
"Please step lively—all aboard."

In just twenty-seven seconds I was on
    the other bank ;
The Committee of Arrangements met me
    on the landing stage—
Knightly Raleigh, Mr. Barnum, princely
    Hamlet, tall and lank,
Shem and Samson, Dr. Johnson and
    Diogenes the sage.

And by these I was escorted to the
    House-boat on the Styx,
Where the shades of every time and
    clime were gathered in great force,
Where they sat about in camp-chairs,
    an anachronistic mix
That split up one's cerebellum like a case
    of real remorse.

Once arrived the function started, Dr.
　　Johnson in the chair,
And he spoke some words of wisdom,
　　most of which I have forgot ;
Then they brought out Jeremiah and he
　　tore his flowing hair
As he let us have a future that was boil-
　　ing pretty hot.

There was nothing that was worthy,
　　there was nothing that was good ;
There was nothing in the future that
　　held anything but woe ;
'Twas an outlook dark and murky as a
　　vast primeval wood ;
And the things we mortals meant for
　　cake were certain to be dough.

There would be no art or letters ; hand-
made verse would not be style ;
And the novels of the future would be
writ by syndicates ;
All the art that men would worship, in
a very little while
Would be fashioned by mechanics with
a store of stencil plates.

There would be no art of cooking, every
man who wished to dine
In the future would be fed by table
d'hotes made up in pills ;
Every man who wanted comfort and
for luxury did pine
As we know it, would find nothing that
could mitigate his ills.

I'll not bore you with the paper in its
    pessimistic length.
It was quite like Jeremiah from begin-
    ning to its close ;
It was full of lamentation, and he wept
    with so much strength
That he nearly swamped the house-boat
    with the tears that swept his nose.

But of course when he had finished he
    received a stunning cheer,
And the spirits all applauded as of
    course they had to do,
As old Jerry left the dais with a smile
    from ear to ear,
With the mild ejaculation "Well, I'm
    mighty glad I'm through."

Then the Doctor spoke more wisdom
for an hour and a half,
While the company all chatted in a very
genial way;
When uprose the sweet Isaiah with a
happy sort of laugh,
And he cast a horoscope that turned old
Jeremiah gray.

It was different from the other in a very
deep-set sense ;
For instead of "sanguinary" it was
"sanguinistic" quite.
All the future would be larksome, all
our joys would be intense,
And the world would banish darkness
and would find its sorrows light.

14

Roses sweet would bloom in winter,
    and the grass would e'er be green
In the face of deadly blizzards and de-
    spite the chilling frost ;
And a smile upon the faces of all people
    would be seen
In a time when not a joy in life by any
    would be lost.

There would be no sore temptations
    and nobody would be sad,
Not a soul would suffer from his woes,
    no one infringe the laws.
All the world would take its lexicons
    and obsolete the bad,
And no man would be a debtor, for we'd
    all be creditors.

All his views were optimistic—and he
    had a deal of wit,
And he had a knack about him that I
    envied—yes I did ;
For his humor was appealing, and it al-
    ways seemed to fit—
He'd a sunshine in his nature of the kind
    that can't be hid !

And of course when he had finished he
    received a stunning cheer,
All the spirits there applauded, as of
    course they had to do;
And Isaiah left the dais with a smile from
    ear to ear,
With the statement that "like Jerry he
    was glad 'twas over, too."

After that with some misgivings, which
    he couldn't well conceal,
Johnson introduced Cassandra "who
    was nothing," so he said,
"But a famous old new woman who'd
    a notion to reveal
In a poem that which to her eyes was
    visible ahead."

Then the Trojan prophetess arose with
    manner full of pride,
And without a single tremor stood and
    looked us in the face.
"I came here to read a poem," she ob-
    served, "but I decide
It were better far to drop a hint to ben-
    fit the race.

"Now I know as well as you do that
 I'm thought to be a wight
Who has not one sixteen-thousandth of
 a right to prophesy,
But as I have sat and listened to the
 prophecies to-night,
It has seemed to me your prophets
 haven't got the eagle eye.

"Jeremiah—dear old fellow !—has ob-
 served that you will find
Everything that stands before you is
 identified with rue.
He has had a vision darksome that unto
 my weakling mind,
Isn't worth a half a ducat, or the breath
 of saying 'Pooh !'

"And Isaiah—charming prophet!—
    sweet Isaiah's quite as bad,
Though we've got to give him credit for
    the picture that he made;
It is truly much more pleasing than a
    vision sore and sad,
But that's where its value ceases, I am
    very much afraid.

" I admit I'm but a woman, but I know
    a thing or two.
I have prophesied for centuries and know
    my trade, I wis.
But there's one thing I must tell you
    that I think you ought to do,
And that is to drop what will be, and
    to think of that which *is*.

" There's no use of speculations such as
  those that we have had.
There's to be no change in nature in the
  coming hundred years.
There'll be just as much of good then in
  proportion to the bad,
There'll be just as much of smiling in
  proportion to the tears.

"We have kept the world agoing for a
  good long bit of time,
And we've found that human nature's
  been the same in every day.
We have listened to forebodings from
  the seers in every clime,
We have looked for the millennium
  that's yet to come our way.

"And despite the evil prophets who
    have cast our horoscope
Full of darkness and of threat'nings, full
    of trouble and of doom,
And despite the sunny prophets who
    have filled our souls with hope
We have found the world unchanging
    in its sunshine and its gloom.

"In the years that stand before us there
    will be no change in this—
Unto some they'll bring all gladness,
    unto others only night ;
Unto all will come not trouble unalloyed,
    nor purest bliss,
As would happen if you prophets who
    have spoken tell us right.

"So instead of reading poems as I stand
  before you now
I advise you steer your house-boat—
  steer it with unceasing care
Through the channel of the present, set
  her overhanging prow
'Twixt Charybdis optimistic and the
  Scylla of despair.

"In conclusion let me tell you that I've
  noticed as a fact—
And I'm getting rather aged, as I think
  you plainly see—
That the man who guides his present
  with a modicum of tact
Won't have any cause to worry over
  that which is to be !

" And the man who takes his bitters as
    they come into his life
And who in the depths of sorrow thinks
    about the good he's had,
I believe will find great comfort in a
    future wherein strife
Is not much in disproportion to the
    things that make him glad."

Now for you, my Psi U. brothers, let
    me write one other line,
To explain if need be why I bring this
    message unto you:
I have promised to be faithful to our
    well beloved shrine,
And I wish to give it all that I have
    found that's good and true.

And in my day I have found it well to
    heed the words of her
Who that night in distant Hades told
    the rules which are the best
To produce the life that's happy, which
    will make your pulses stir
As you realize e'en in your woes how
    greatly you are blest !

And as fair Cassandra said to us, so say
    I to you now ;
When embarking on the sea of life,
    steer with unceasing care
Through the channel of the present,
    keep your vessel with its prow
'Twixt Charybdis optimistic and the
    Scylla of despair!

A PLEA FOR NATURALISM

WRITTEN FOR THE LITERARY EXERCISES
OF THE PSI UPSILON FRATERNITY
CONVENTION: NEW YORK
APRIL THE SEVENTH
MDCCCXCII

THE day was well nigh spent; the
    noon of night
Was soon to show the dying year its
    grave,
And merry chimes, impatient to accord
A welcome to the new, scarce held their
    tongues
In decent silence until all was o'er.
The outer world, that in the times of old

Was used to lie beneath a robe of white,
Lay cold and still and gray—a symbol
fit,
A symbol of a dying child of time
Whose course was run; while here and
there there peeped
Up through the hardened crust of
Mother Earth
A bit of green, which seemed a promise
sweet
Of blest eternity; since none shall die
Whose dying moments are not soothed
with hope
That there are others on whose shoul-
ders strong
The burdens grown too great to bear
shall fall,
And falling, find their Atlas there.
                         Within

The embers glowed, and by their light
    I sat,

A watcher, sad, alone ; the coming year

Was but a hope, the present was but
    death.

I could not join with them that feasted
    then,

For watch-night revelries bring to my
    mind

The sin of Gertrude and that Danish
    King,

When meats prepared for festival of woe

Were set scarce cold to deck a marriage
    feast.

As was my wont I mused upon the past,

Revolving o'er and o'er the joys and
    griefs

Of this, the year whose knell should
    soon be tolled.

A casting of accounts it was to see
If good or ill were measured out the
more ;
And as I mused, I saw where Nature
took
All undeterred her course, life seemed
most sweet,
While what of woe had been therein for
man
Had come from acts rebellious to her
rule.

Then suddenly, afar, across the hills
The midnight bells began their solemn
dirge—
A dirge that, as its slow and measured
tones
Rang sadly out upon the crisp night air,

28

Should swell into an Ave, thus to greet
The advent of the new-born year. The
    strokes
As each one fell upon my ear I strove
To count, when on a sudden all was still;
The air was scarcely vibrant with the
    sixth
When Time itself a moment seemed to
    pause.
My soul was awed; in wonderment my
    eyes
Roved over all, and with my ears attent
I listened for the strokes completing
    twelve ;
And as I listened then there came a
    sound
As of the voice of one of wisdom ripe
Addressing one he loved, in whom his
    hope

Was centered—words a dying father
    might
Have whispered to a well-beloved son.

And, as the words came, I could see two
    forms:
Upon my right a sturdy youth there
    sat,
Who gazed in rapt attention on the face
Of him who spoke ; the speaker, bent
    with age,
His patriarchal beard snow white, his
    eye,
Which dissolution soon should glaze,
    most bright,
Sat to the left of me—the meeting 'twas
Of him whose work was done and that
    one who

Was now to take his place—of one who
    saw
Wherein his failures lay, and now had
    come
To point another to the path of Truth ;
And, tremulously voiced, his words
    were these :
"This is an age of artifice, my son—
An age wherein the artificial stands
More honored far than that which
    Nature makes—
A lesson I have learned in bitterness.
When, one long year agone, I stood as
    you
Now stand upon the threshold of your
    time,
No one was there to indicate to me
Where pitfalls lay, and to direct my
    thoughts

To channels which should upward lead
   mankind.
I had no mentor, boy, to give to me,
As I now give to you, one hint of that
Surpassing opportunity, now lost,
To lead man back from those unstable
   heights
From which he now looks down upon
   the plain
Where Nature rests—back to her loving
   arms
Who is the mother blest of every good—
Back from the clouds of unreality
Into the world that breathes the living
   God.
In letters what do men to-day ? They
   wield
A marvelously pretty pen ; their works
Voluminous and graceful multiply,

Upbuilding monuments—of thought?
   Ah, no !
But shafts of words in memory of Style—
Mosaics with surpassing beauty
   phrased—
But yet as hard, and cold, and void of
   truth
As any stone-depicted scene must be.
In poetry we find most tender hearts
Engaged with pretty thoughts as like
   to those
Of Shakespeare and of Milton as the
   lakes
That snuggle in the mountain fastnesses
Are like the broad and unrestrainèd
   sea ;
Their days are spent confining flies of
   thought
In deep and mellow amber cages till

You're conscious of the amber—not the
fly.

Blind worshippers of form are they—of
form

Man-made, and not that wondrous,
beautiful,

Though shapeless seeming form that
bears the stamp

Which shows it heaven sent—sweet
Nature's own ;

Of form which drives from great to little
things,

Destroys man's potency to move the
heart,

And gives instead a fleeting thrill to
sense ;

Of form which holds in bondage genius
e'en,

So that our poets, e'en the most inspired,

34

Seem rhymesters of the garden close
    and not
The minstrels of the hills, the wilder-
    ness,
Who sing the Anthems of the Universe.
Our novelists, when they essay the real,
Are bound to be romancers all, because
The ways of man so artificial are
They have no slightest semblance to
    that mode
Of living here which Nature would
    prescribe.
In artifice are all things reared ; by it
Are all things formed—nor matters it
    one jot
Where you may look, that most ac-
    cursed taint
Of so-called art hath sicklied o'er all
    things

With that most dreadful pallor which
    precedes
No less a thing than death.   Man can-
    not live
In insincerity always ; no more
Can aught else in the universe exist
Which most persistent everywhere
    pursues
That corruscating will-o'-wisp, Untruth.
Our painters, would they be content to
    tread
Where Nature leads, her followers
    become,
Might take us back to those immortal
    days
When masters were ; when it were
    heresy
For mortal hands e'en to so much as
    hint

That Nature might do better could she
    see
Through mortal eyes ; why, boy, but
    yesterday
I saw a canvas by a man of fame
Depicting scenes he never saw, effects
Of so-called light and color which have
    come
From nothing less than dreams induced
    by strong
Potations in a mind diseased, malformed.
And on their knees before this self-same
    work,
The critics worshipped and its author
    hailed
As one inspired—as one to whom was
    sent
A gift divine from God on high. The
    gift

Was God's, the instrument, alas ! was
    weak.
A chosen soul intrusted with His work
Was swerved from duty's path and
    made to lie
Prostrate before this Juggernaut of Art !
The stage hath artifice unspeakable.
And in the mart men purchase and then
    sell
For uncoined, undiscoverable gold,
Unplanted grains and non-existent
    shares.
'Tis found in churches—day by day we
    seem
To wander farther from the simplest
    truths ;
We're so befogged by articles of faith,
By dogmas of the church, things
    orthodox,

That worthy spirits choose the simplest
  texts
And cover reams of paper to explain
What should be patent to the weakest
  mind—
Not only should, but would be patent
  had
Man made one slightest effort to retain
Their sweet simplicity, and to prevent
The priests of Sect, of Form, of Artifice
From weaving round about them till
  obscure
The web of Dogma, Satan's own
  device.
In life political not conscience rules;
Expediency, artifice, holds sway,
And nations find themselves divided on
The problems which the plainest com-
  mon sense,

Plus honesty, could in one moment
    solve :
And they who seek our highest offices
Must bend before machines—those
    Frankensteins
Of politics, which ever sacrifice
The country's good to politicians' greed,
And conscience withers 'neath ambi-
    tion's lust.
The remedy ? 'Tis Nature—that is all.
Let Nature once again assert her power :
Let Nature say to man, ' 'Tis mine to
    rule,
Thine to obey,' and it is done—and once
'Tis done, man hath an ally to insure
Complete attainment of his cherished
    ends ;
And messages of God through mortals
    sent

Will surer reach their destination here,
Will surer reach the hearts of those
    whose place
In meekness 'tis to listen, not to lead.
And ere I leave thee, boy, I beg thee
    take
The words of one who's learned the
    truth to heart.
And let it be thy task to show to him
Who follows after thee the work begun
Of reinstating Nature on her throne;
Of placing man where he should be—
    below,
And not above.   Not this for Nature's
    sake,
But that usurping man himself may take
That lofty place in this grand universe
Which will be his if he but choose
    aright

The path thereto—'neath Nature's guiding hand."

The bells, resuming, tolled the seventh
stroke,
And on the eighth the youth rose up and
strode
To where the old man sat ; then, kneeling there,
He kissed his hand. The other sadly
smiled ;
The forehead of the youth he kissed,
and as
The last completing stroke of twelve
rang out,
Passed from my sight. Again was I
alone ;
Yet not alone, for with me rested HOPE.

42

www.ingramcontent.com/pod-product-compliance
Lightning Source LLC
Chambersburg PA
CBHW021429090426
42739CB00009B/1408